Who is this booklet for?

This booklet is for parents of students taking GCSE exams.

How can it help?

The aims of this booklet are:

✓ To give you an insight into what students do when they revise.

✓ To give you lots of tips, suggestions and ideas about how you can support your child with their revision.

✓ To boost your confidence in the role you take during the revision and exam period.

Contents

Using this Booklet	2
What is My Role as a Parent?	3
Getting Started	4
1. Motivation	5
2. Revision Planning	8
3. Revision Sessions	13
4. Revision and Memory	17
5. Thorny Issues	23
6. The Reluctant Student	26
7. Exam Stress	27
8. Sitting Exams	30
Revision Timetable Pull-out	centre pages

Using This Booklet

- The intention behind this booklet is not to give you a foolproof master plan but to provide you with a whole heap of tips, suggestions and ideas for you to consider.

- ***Do not attempt to put all these suggestions into practice as this would be totally unrealistic (and exhausting!). Pick out just a few ideas that you feel could work for you and your child.***

- What works fantastically well for some will be a complete disaster for others and so the approach is more 'pick-and-mix' than 'one-size-fits-all'.

- ***There is no correct way to be a parent in this situation but this booklet aims to help you to make the most of the approach which best suits you, your child and your situation.***

Do

✓ Flick through the booklet to see what each of the sections is about.
✓ Try out and adapt any ideas that appeal to you.
✓ Keep this booklet in a handy place throughout the revision period and dip into it from time to time.
✓ Have a pen or highlighter handy as you are reading and highlight the ideas you like as you go along.

Don't

✗ Use any suggestions that you feel are unsuitable in your situation.
✗ Stop using any of your own ideas and approaches if they have worked for you and your child in the past.
✗ Read the booklet through from start to finish but dip into it to look at topics that are of interest to you.

What is My Role as a Parent?

- Success in exams is a team effort which involves you, the school and your child working together and so you will play a variety of roles.

- A key role is to support the work of the school as, like you, they only want the best for your child. By having a positive relationship with the school you are playing a vital role in helping your child to achieve their potential.

- At home you will probably play a number of roles which may include cheerleader, counsellor, motivator, coach, information gatherer, project manager and supplies co-ordinator!

- This is a stressful and emotionally charged period for you, your child and your family so you can expect drastic mood swings and unexpected behaviour. One of your most important roles is to make home life as calm and supportive as possible.

- In this role you are not expected to fully understand the details of the exam system, know anything about sitting exams or be an expert in any subjects but your input will still make a huge difference!

6 Ideas To Get You Started

OK. Take a deep breath. Here goes…..

1 **Take a few moments to think about what your role might be during the revision period and how you might be able to support your child.**

2 Make a point of discussing with your child what will be involved in the revision period and what your role could be. It's probably best to do this early on before routines and habits are formed.

3 Respond positively when they ask you to help, ask exactly how you can help and if you can't help immediately say when it's convenient.

4 Be prepared to be told that your help is not required (this can be disheartening) - but don't take this to mean that you shouldn't do anything at all.

5 Try to attend all parents' consultation evenings and any exam-related information evenings. Read any information the school sends out in the form of letters, newsletters, booklets etc or which are posted on the school website.

6 If you are in any doubt about anything to do with revision and the exams contact the relevant subject teacher, Form Tutor or Head of Year at school. *Teachers are incredibly busy people but have a very real passion for wanting each and every student to achieve their best and will welcome you contacting them.*

1

✓ How Parents Can Help with
MOTIVATION

Key points:
- ▶ Students are motivated to do well in their GCSEs by a variety of reasons – there is no correct reason.
- ▶ Students with a strong reason for wanting to do well in their GCSEs generally find it easier to get down to study.
- ▶ Your interest, support and encouragement can play a key role in helping your child to establish and maintain their motivation.

Take an interest

Perhaps the most important thing you can do to help your child to stay motivated during the revision period is to express an interest in what they're doing.

- ✓ Ask about their plans for revision, how they feel things are going, what's working well and what they're having problems with.
- ✓ Look for opportunities to praise them for their efforts.
- ✓ Encourage them to believe in themselves by reminding them of things they have done well in the past.

Target grades

Every student is set a target grade in each subject and these are usually given in progress reports issued by their school. Many students find it motivational to work towards reaching or exceeding these target grades. A new grading scale of 9 to 1 is now being used, with 9 being the top grade.

✓ *Talk with your child about what grades they expect to get in different subjects.*
✓ *Discuss how challenging or easy these target grades are.*
✓ *Ask them which subjects they want to do particularly well in and in which subjects they want to achieve higher than the target grade.*
✓ *Have realistic expectations of what they are likely to achieve.*

> "Try to make sure your expectations are realistic."

Why am I doing this?

It's a great advantage if your child is clear about their reasons for doing well in their GCSEs. These reasons might include short term goals such as getting into the Sixth Form or College or longer term goals such as going to university, doing an apprenticeship, a future career or satisfying job, a dream lifestyle, or simply earning lots of money at some later stage!

✓ *Discuss with your child what they want to do after their GCSEs.*
✓ *Make sure they are clear about the grades they need to get into Sixth Form/College or to pursue a particular career.*
✓ *Throughout Year 10 and Year 11 encourage them to make the most of work experience opportunities, to attend careers events and to talk to teachers about career pathways.*
✓ *Get them to book a careers interview with the school careers adviser.*
✓ *When possible, get family and friends to talk to them about their own education experiences and jobs.*

Incentives and rewards

The issue of whether to offer rewards or incentives is hotly debated. For most students, wanting to get good grades, a place in Sixth Form/College or the prospect of a future career is sufficient motivation.

However, some students do respond well to other incentives such as the promise of buying something for them, taking them to a place/event once the exams are over or financial incentives. These incentives may be linked to just one subject, a number of subjects or all subjects.

✓ *Before embarking on this approach think about whether offering incentives will really increase the effort your child will put in.*
✓ *If you do decide to go down this route, discuss with your child what sort of rewards would motivate them and how to make the targets realistic but also sufficiently challenging.*
✓ *Instead of offering an incentive based on their results you could offer something as a treat after their exams regardless of how well they do.*

Normal life will return....

GCSEs are very important but after the exams things will get back to normal and your child will have several months off to relax and enjoy themselves before starting Sixth Form or College.

✓ *Remind them from time-to-time that the exams will not go on forever. You may want to remind yourself of this fact too!*
✓ *Have something for them to look forward to once the exams are all over such as an evening out, weekend away, holiday, visit to their favourite restaurant, trip to a theme park or whatever takes their fancy.*

"Remind them that normal life will return!"

2

✓ How Parents Can Help with
REVISION PLANNING

> ### Key points:
> ▶ There is no escaping the fact that revising for GCSE exams involves many hours of personal study.
> ▶ Their final grades will not only depend on how many hours of revision they do but also how well they use this time.
> ▶ Revision plans are very individual and vary enormously but will usually involve some sort of routine and/or a timetable.

It's never too soon to make a start!

There is no 'correct' time to start revising, this will depend on the individual student and the guidance they are given by their school. The sooner your child starts revising the less daunting it will be.

Most schools have mock exams (sometimes called Pre-Public Exams or PPEs) in November or December. The results from these will give your child some idea of how well they're doing and what they still need to work on. They also provide a great opportunity for your child to practise their revision techniques.

Many Year 11 students will start revising for their final exams as early as January/February and 'full-on' revision should start at the beginning of the Easter holidays. The reason for starting so early is that there is two years of study to cover and assessment for most subjects is by exam only.

> *"Encourage them to treat mock exams seriously."*

✓ *Ask their teachers what guidance they have given about when to start revising and how many hours a night/week they suggest.*
✓ *Ensure that your child has a copy of their examination timetable - make a copy of this just in case it gets mislaid.*
✓ *If you have a calendar in the kitchen write the exam dates on it.*
✓ *Encourage them to treat mock exams seriously and to revise for them.*

What to revise?

Before your child starts revising they need to make sure that they have a complete set of notes for each subject as they probably will have been absent from school from time to time.

For each subject, it is useful if they have a list of the topics they have covered and they can then decide in what order to tackle the topics. They don't have to revise the topics in exactly the same order in which they were taught and it's a good idea to pick a topic they like or find easy to start with as this boosts their confidence. It's also probably a good idea to revise early on topics they were taught at the beginning of their courses as some of these will be a bit hazy!

Students need to be careful that they don't spend too much time on subjects they like or are good at and neglect their less favoured subjects. It should be noted that most topics they study will have to be revised more than once and often several times before the information sinks in.

✓ Get them to check that all their class notes are up to date, with no gaps.
✓ If they are unsure about the topics they have studied, suggest they ask their subject teachers for a list.
✓ Encourage them to work on their weaknesses and the subjects/topics they don't like as well as the subjects/topics they like and are good at.

It's always better to have a plan

You may hear your child say things like "Plans don't work for me, I have to be in the mood to revise" but this approach usually leads to very little revision being done. Revision planning, when done realistically, helps to ensure that the necessary hours of revision actually take place.

Making revision plans is also useful for helping your child to get a good balance between revision and leisure time. It is very important that they take time off from their studies to relax, so don't expect them to study all the time or every day of the week.

✓ Discuss and agree such things as an appropriate balance between revision and social life.
✓ Encourage them to continue meeting up with their friends and to attend their usual clubs and societies.
✓ Be flexible if something special comes along such as celebrating a friend's birthday.
✓ Allow them occasionally to miss a pre-planned revision session.

Revision planning: During term time

On school days, the best way to ensure a regular amount of revision gets done is if your child follows some sort of routine. A study routine simply involves them starting and finishing at roughly the same times each day. The amount of independent revision they get done on any particular day will vary according to how much homework they also have to do.

The exact times they start and finish will depend on a number of factors such as the time they get home from school, whether they prefer to relax for a bit before getting down to their studies and what happens around mealtimes in your house.

When they come home from school and are ready to start studying, students should spend 5-10 minutes making a quick plan for that evening. This should involve giving some thought to which subjects to revise, for how long, when to take breaks and when to finish, taking into account mealtimes and not forgetting any homework.

✓ Ask if they would like you to help them set up a daily routine.
✓ Discuss with them the possible timings of a routine.
✓ Pin up the times of their revision routine in a place everyone in the house can see and wherever possible try to support this routine.
✓ When they get home from school encourage them to make a list of the subjects they are going to revise for that evening.

Revision planning: During school holidays

"Help them set up a daily revision routine."

During school holidays there is potentially far more time available for revision than on normal school days. The Easter and May half-term breaks offer your child a great opportunity to put in a good number of hours of revision (holidays also give them the perfect chance to lounge around in bed too!). A different approach is suggested for holidays which involves making a revision timetable where the subjects to revise are planned in advance, usually for the week ahead.

Revision planning can be done using printed revision timetable templates, an example of which can be found in the centre pages of this booklet, and a variety of formats are readily available online. Apps are also available for creating personalised revision timetables.

If you are going to be involved in helping your child to draw up a revision timetable, try using these steps:

Step 1 Remove the timetable pull-out from the centre pages of this booklet. It's double-sided so choose which format your child likes best (or use a different template or app).

Step 2 Ask your child to make a list of all their subjects.

Step 3 Get them to write in all non-school commitments for that week such as leisure activities, going out, seeing friends, time to relax etc.

Step 4 Get them to enter when to revise each subject for that week, keeping in mind the following ideas:
- balance the revision time between subjects
- space out the revision for each subject over the week
- vary the subjects revised on each day

Step 5 Now pin up the revision timetable in a prominent place at home so that everyone in the house knows what's going on.

✓ *Ask if they would like you to help them to draw up a revision timetable or whether they would prefer to do this alone.*
✓ *If you are asked for your input, help them to create a plan which is realistic and which they can stick to.*
✓ *Don't impose a revision timetable on them as this is unlikely to work.*
✓ *Don't expect them to study all the time as taking time out to relax will have a positive effect on their work.*

3

✓ How Parents Can Help with
REVISION SESSIONS

> ### Key points:
> ▶ A successful revision session is one where a solid amount of work gets done.
> ▶ It is important that students structure their revision sessions to ensure concentration levels are kept high.
> ▶ Having a suitable place to study at home is important during the revision period.

Revision resources

Your child will need a variety of books, stationery and equipment before they start the final revision push.

✓ Make sure they have all the basic equipment such as pens, pencils, ruler, a protractor, a compass, calculator, A4 writing pads, clear pencil case for exams.

✓ Other things which are useful to buy include record cards, highlighters, coloured pens/pencils, folder dividers, sticky notes, kitchen timer.

✓ Ask them if they need any subject specific study or revision guides.

Working environment

"Try to make sure they have a quiet place to study at home."

Your child will spend many hours revising at school, both in normal lessons and during extra revision sessions held after school, but it's the extra time they spend revising independently at home that can make such a big difference.

Ideally, when they are studying at home, they need a permanent, quiet, well-lit place to study with very few interruptions or distractions. The best set up is probably to have a flat surface such a desk or table in their bedroom. The problem with using other spaces, such as the living room or kitchen, is that they are more likely to be interrupted from their studies.

However, students like to work in difference places in different ways and working at a desk or table isn't always possible, practical or even preferable. Instead, some students do like to work in the kitchen or living room or if they do study in their bedroom prefer to lie on their bed rather than sit at a desk.

When studying, they should make sure that the desk or table they are working at is clear of everything except for relevant material and equipment and free from anything that might distract them. It is a good idea for them to get into the habit of tidying up their workspace at the end of each revision session so that it is clear when they start again.

- ✓ *Ask your child if they think they have a suitable working environment at home and what you can do to improve things.*
- ✓ *Make sure that siblings and anyone else in the house are aware that they will need to be extra considerate at this time.*
- ✓ *If it proves difficult to find a suitable place to revise at home, find out if their school offers quiet spaces before or after school or during lunch breaks.*

Revise, test, rest

Revision sessions should be kept to a reasonable length and anywhere between 1-3 hours is about right, with regular short breaks. Before starting a revision session, students need to set a definite time to start and finish and stick to it.

An effective revision session follows a pattern of revise, test, rest and might be divided up like this: 40 minutes revising, 10 minutes testing, 10 minutes resting or 20 minutes revising, 5 minutes testing, 5 minutes resting.

Short bursts of revision following this pattern can be useful when students are tired or the topic is difficult or boring. They should always try to end each revision session by summing up or testing.

Many students like to have something to look forward to or some kind of reward after a revision session. This might include spending time on their phone, watching videos or a favourite snack.

✓ *Offer to help them to structure their revision sessions.*
✓ *Ask if they would like you to help with testing them at the end of revision periods.*
✓ *Buy a cheap digital kitchen timer so that they can keep track of time during revision sessions and take scheduled breaks.*

✓ If you notice that they keep interrupting their studies by going to get food or drink, offer to bring them a snack at a convenient time.
✓ Dehydration can reduce mental performance so make sure they have a bottle of water nearby.
✓ Think about a simple treat you could give them after a revision session.

I'm bored now!

The best way for your child to keep concentration levels high is to take regular breaks. How often and for how long these breaks are will depend on how long they are revising for, the material they are revising, the time of day and their own concentration span. A good guide is that for every hour they work they should have a break of 10 minutes, although they may find that a break after every 20 or 30 minutes works best.

If your child finds it difficult to concentrate for long periods of time they should start with short sessions and gradually build up to longer sessions. Varying the topic or the subject during each revision session may also help them to concentrate for longer. Remember, they need to build concentration stamina as some exams are over 2 hours long.

Most students are at their best in the morning (though not everyone!), so on days when they are studying at home for long periods such as weekends or holidays they could try working on difficult topics in the morning when their mind is fresher.

✓ Help them to find out which subjects they prefer to revise when they get home from school and which can be planned for later in the evening.
✓ Encourage your child to have regular, short breaks and don't expect them to study for hours on end.
✓ Get them to recognise when they are 'zoning out' (this may not be time related) and to respond to this by changing subject/activity.

THU	FRI	SAT	SUN

Weekly Revision Timetable

	MON	TUE	WED
8-9			
9-10			
10-11			
11-12			
12-1			
1-2			
2-3			
3-4			
4-5			
5-6			
6-7			
7-8			
8-9			
9-10			

THU	FRI	SAT	SUN

Weekly Revision Timetable

	MON	TUE	WED
Morning			
Afternoon			
Evening			

4

✓ How Parents Can Help with
REVISING and MEMORY

Key points:
▶ Revising actively is the best way to make sense of the material being studied and also helps to remember it.
▶ Just reading through class notes is a very poor revision method.
▶ Tackling past papers and exam-type questions is essential.

So what is revision?

The purpose of revision is to reinforce what students already know and to find out and then learn what they don't know.

There are many different ways to revise and your child will probably have their own preferred methods. These methods are likely to vary from subject to subject.

All revision should be done with the final exam for that subject in mind and should focus on the type of questions that will be asked on exam papers. You may hear your child say that you can't revise for certain subjects but this is most definitely not the case. There is no exam or part of any exam that can't be revised for in some way.

✓ Encourage your child to try out different revision techniques so that they can find out which methods work best for them.
✓ If they don't understand something or are unsure how to revise a particular subject encourage them to ask a teacher.
✓ Try not to relate too much to how you did your revision!

Revision classes

All schools run a variety of revision classes which are in addition to normal lessons. These classes may take place before school, during lunchtime, after school, Saturday mornings or during school holidays.

Revision classes provide a great opportunity for your child to ask about topics they are struggling with and to pick up extra tips on exam technique.

✓ Strongly encourage your child to attend these revision classes and any other revision activities organised by the school.
✓ Suggest that they take along topics they are finding difficult.

Revision guides

Most students find revision guides very helpful for revision. When buying a revision guide, make sure it is the correct one for the exam board they are using (and the most up-to-date version) and that they like the style it's written in. It is quite likely that their subject teachers will recommend a particular publisher.

"When buying revision guides, check the exam board."

The internet provides students with access to a huge variety of excellent revision resources (notes, videos, past papers, apps, quizzes etc) but be aware that some of these resources may not be relevant.

✓ For each subject get your child to ask their teacher to recommend useful revision guides, websites and apps.

✓ At parents' evenings ask teachers which online learning resources and apps the school provides for students and how to access them.

✓ When buying revision guides check that it is for the relevant exam board (and in some subjects whether foundation or higher tier).

Testing, testing

The key to remembering important facts, formulae, definitions, quotations, theories and ideas is repeated testing. The more a student practices recalling information, the more likely they will remember it in the long term and the more confident they will feel about their ability to remember.

The great thing about testing is that it is an ideal way for you to help them and can be done in short bursts. You might find yourself testing them from their own revision notes, revision notes provided by their teachers or information they have found in a revision guide, website or app.

✓ Volunteer your services for testing on a regular basis.

✓ Testing is such a great way to help your child with their revision that it is worth a second mention!

✓ Or get them to 'teach' you a topic so that you understand it. You could find yourself learning about bioloeaching in Chemistry, pyramidal peaks in Geography or Fartlek training in PE!

Revise in a flash!

Writing revision notes is a great way of being active and your child will find this method useful for any subject where facts need to be remembered. Writing revision notes involves picking out the most important points and trying to reduce the amount of information to a more manageable amount.

Revision notes can be written anywhere but many students like to use flash cards (also called file cards or record cards).

Flashcards are great because they can be carried around in a pocket or bag and contain only a small amount of information, so they aren't so daunting to learn from.

A very effective way of writing flash cards is as questions and answers, where a question (or questions) is written on one side of the card and the corresponding answer(s) on the reverse side.

✓ *Buy them some flash cards (available from supermarkets, stationery stores or online in a variety of sizes and colours).*
✓ *Offer to test your child using the flash cards they have written.*

Exam papers and exam board websites

Revision isn't just about learning facts. It's also vital that students are able to use this knowledge to answer exam questions and so tackling past or sample exam papers is a great way to improve their exam technique.

Tackling exam papers is also a great way for students to identify gaps in their learning. Once they have identified a topic they struggle with they can then revise it before tackling more exam questions on the same topic to see if they've closed the gap in their learning (see below).

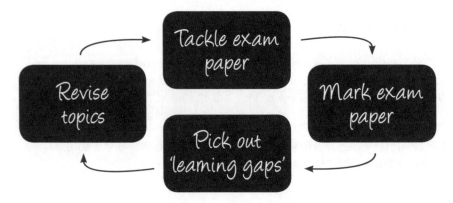

Some of your child's revision time should be devoted to practising under exam conditions. This means putting away books and trying out sample questions as if they were in the exam. This should get them used to working at high speed for long periods of time because that's what they'll be doing in most exams.

Each exam board has its own website where you can find and download past papers. There are several different exam boards and your child will probably be taking GCSE subjects from at least two of them.

Exam board websites also contain a lot of other very useful information on each subject including the specification (a list of the topics they need to learn), mark schemes for past papers and grade boundaries (a new grading scale of 9 to 1 is now being used, with 9 being the top grade).

Looking at exam board websites can be a little confusing because, in addition to the information on current GCSEs, they also still have information on old-style or 'legacy' exams (where grades A*-G are used).

✓ *Encourage them to look at the exam board website for past papers and mark schemes.*
✓ *When you go to Parents' Evenings ask each subject teacher for the name of the exam board they are following in that subject.*
✓ *Also ask if your child is doing foundation or higher tier (this only applies in certain subjects).*

Making your house a 'revision zone'

Many students go way beyond using the standard methods of using flash cards, study guides and revision websites and use parts of the house as a 'revision zone'. Some students like to write key points on sticky notes and stick them to things like bathroom mirrors, toilet doors, stair banisters, kitchen cupboards, fridges and so on (are you ready for this?!).

However, the place they are most likely to use as a 'revision zone' is their own bedroom and students can be very creative about the places they choose to display revision notes! Some students like to plaster every part of their bedroom with a vast array of notes from different subjects whilst others do this on a smaller scale and focus only on a small number of things they are struggling to remember.

Other approaches include hanging large sheets of paper or even old wallpaper on walls, sticking flash cards on the ceiling, using dry wipe noticeboards, magnetic whiteboards or corkboards (it could get messy!).

✓ *It's probably best to have a quick word with them about using your house and their bedroom as a 'revision zone'!*
✓ *Buy them any additional items they need eg whiteboard, old wallpaper, display magnets, large size sticky notes etc.*

And there's more!

Whilst revision notes, testing and tackling past exam papers are the core staples of revision, there is a huge variety of other ways in which students revise for exams.

"Don't compare their revision methods to the ones you used."

Other approaches may include making up songs or rhymes, chanting, creating silly memory links, using apps to make up quizzes, recording key points on a phone, drawing cartoons, revision sessions with friends, audio downloads, podcasts – there is no 'correct' way to revise.

✓ *Be positive if your child uses unfamiliar or unusual revision methods.*
✓ *Don't compare the methods they use with any that you or their siblings may have used in the past.*

5

✓ How Parents Can Help with
THORNY ISSUES

Key points:
▶ You can expect some difficult issues to crop up during the revision period.
▶ These issues can be the source of a lot of disagreement and friction between parents and children.
▶ When addressing these issues try to avoid arguments.

Thorny issue 1: TV or not TV?

This is pretty straightforward. Under no circumstances should a student revise in front of the TV or when streaming videos on a device. The only exception is if they are watching a revision video.

✓ *Insist they don't revise in front of the TV.*

Thorny issue 2: Problems with ping!

If you hear a constant ping! ping! ping! when they are studying, it's time to intervene. Revising whilst at the same time checking social media, texting, instant messaging or watching video clips are not compatible activities. When revising, your child needs to find a way of avoiding constantly checking their phone.

The simplest way to do this is for them to put their phone (and possibly other devices) in a different room where the temptation is out of the way – and to put it on silent!

✓ *If they constantly check their phone when revising, discuss ways they can avoid doing this.*

Thorny issue 3: Sound of silence

Students listen to music in a variety of ways and for different reasons so this is not as clear cut an issue as TV or phones. Some students say it helps with their concentration whilst others use earphones to block out background noise.

Attempting to memorise facts and information or working through exam papers under exam conditions should be done in silence. If occasionally students are going to listen to music, it should be played at low volume and they should choose something that doesn't distract them. If they find themselves singing along, then they are distracted!

✓ *Encourage them to be selective about what they listen to and to work in silence for memorising and doing practice exam papers.*
✓ *Don't make a battle out of whether or not they listen to music when doing their revision.*

Thorny issue 4: Screening out

If they are using a tablet or laptop for revision they will have to exercise some self-discipline. If they have social media apps on their device it's going to be difficult for them to resist the temptation to respond to every message, notification or alert they might get.

✓ *Suggest they don't leave social media tabs or apps open and when watching videos use full screen to avoid clicking on other links.*

Thorny issue 5 – And so to bed

Having a good night's sleep is vital when studying hard, so having a regular time when they switch off lights and sleep is important.

It is also important that they do something when they have finished studying for the evening to help them relax such as catching up with friends on social media, watching videos/TV, reading, listening to music, gaming etc.

However, whilst spending time on social media or a games console is fine for a limited amount of time, staying up half the night messaging or gaming should definitely be avoided!

✓ *Discuss a regular time for lights out.*
✓ *Suggest that they leave time after studying to wind down.*
✓ *Be flexible with the lights out time at weekends and for special events.*

Thorny issue 6 – Don't compare!

There is nothing more guaranteed to irritate your child and cause tension between you than to make comparisons with other people's revision methods or routines.

They really won't want to hear that you remembered key facts by changing the words to your favourite songs (even if it worked), that an older sibling used to get up at the crack of dawn to study (even if they did) or that a friend's child is able to revise for 5 hours at a stretch without a break (they probably can't)!

> *"Don't make comparisons with your child's siblings or friends."*

✓ *Whenever you feel yourself about to make a comparison just STOP!*

6

✓ How Parents Can Help with

The RELUCTANT STUDENT

Some students just don't want to revise and you will meet a brick wall of resistance. There are no easy solutions but here are some suggestions:

✓ *Maintain an active interest in what they are doing throughout the revision and exam period.* **Ask them what help you can give and to let you know if they want anything. Keep encouraging them and giving gentle reminders but without getting on their nerves!**

✓ *Encourage them to go along to revision classes and other interventions run by their teachers.* **Contact the school to find out when revision sessions are held for different subjects.**

You never know what might be the key to holding their attention."

✓ *Make revision at home active by offering to test them. Get them to read through a short section from an exercise book or revision guide and ask questions about it or help them make notes.* **You never know what might be the key to holding their attention.**

✓ *Avoid detailed revision timetables but instead help them to decide what to revise and when to revise on a day-to-day basis.* **Suggest that they revise in short bursts of 15-20 minutes at a time.**

7

✓ How Parents Can Help with

EXAM STRESS

> **Key points:**
> ▶ *All students feel a degree of stress over the exam period.*
> ▶ *There are many simple ways to reduce this stress.*
> ▶ *You have a vital role to play in helping your child deal with exam stress.*

What to expect

It is quite normal if your child is anxious about their exams but some find it harder to cope with the pressure than others. They may well want to talk more than usual about their feelings, thoughts and fears during this period but equally may choose not to discuss things at all.

Your child needs to feel you are supportive of their efforts regardless of the results they achieve and from time to time they will need to be reassured of this support.

> ✓ *Make sure you are available to listen to your child, although they may not want to talk directly about exams.*
> ✓ *Expect to encounter wild swings in their moods and uncharacteristic outbursts during the lead up to exams.*

✓ If things aren't going well in a particular subject, arrange to visit the
school to talk to the teacher concerned or make contact by email.
✓ Look out for signs of unhealthy levels of stress and if they are not coping
contact the school or visit your GP.

Revision planning

A major source of stress for
students is the feeling that they
are unprepared and haven't done
enough revision. It is unsurprising
that most students feel this way
as potentially there is an endless amount of revision to be done.

"Help them to make a realistic revision timetable."

Revision plans (take a look at pages 8-12) can help to reduce feelings of
anxiety students may have and following through on these plans helps to
boost confidence in their ability to do well in the exams.

However, some of the most conscientious and hard-working students also
suffer from feeling that they aren't doing enough and need to be encouraged
to take time off. A major benefit of having a revision plan is that social and
leisure activities are included in the schedule.

✓ Help your child to draw up and keep to a realistic revision plan.
✓ Encourage them to build social, leisure and sport activities into the plan.
✓ If things aren't going to plan, offer your assistance in helping to put things
back on track.
✓ Don't nag about domestic tasks such as tidying their bedroom, helping
around the house or tidying up after themselves!
✓ Be flexible about whether they attend family events.

Healthy body, healthy mind

Eating well reduces the overall stress on the body and can also make a person feel good about themselves. Exercising helps to clear the mind and provides a way of releasing a great deal of the muscle tension which stress produces.

✓ *Provide your child with a variety of healthy meals.*
✓ *Encourage them to exercise.*
✓ *Encourage them to drink lots of water.*

Thinking positively

You may well hear your child constantly say negative things such as "I'm going to fail" or "There just isn't enough time". Too many negative thoughts can adversely affect your child's self-belief and you may need to help your child replace these with more positive thoughts.

✓ *If your child is constantly saying negative things, find something positive to say about the way they are working.*
✓ *Look for ways in which you can help them to believe in themselves by reminding them of any successes they have had.*
✓ *Get them to focus on the short-term task of revising rather than thinking about the final results.*

Keeping things in perspective

Whilst GCSE exams are undoubtedly important, if for some reason your child doesn't get the grades they had hoped for it is not the end of the world. They may have to rethink their immediate plans for what to do in Sixth Form/College (although entry criteria can be flexible) but a huge variety of opportunities will be still be open to them.

✓ *Help them to keep things in perspective by looking at the 'bigger picture'.*

8

✓ How Parents Can Help with

SITTING EXAMS

> **Key points:**
> ▶ The period around the time of the exams is the most stressful for your
>   child - and for you.
> ▶ The day of an exam can be a particularly anxious time.
> ▶ Emotions after exams vary considerably.

The night before an exam

The night before an exam, students should only attempt light revision
using revision notes and not try to do any totally new revision. This does,
of course, depend on whether they have been revising hard in the weeks
leading up to the exam!

They will need to get together all the necessary equipment (pens, rulers,
calculators etc plus spares) in a clear pencil case as the last thing they want
in the morning is to be rushing around trying to find things. It might be a
good idea to have a back-up pencil case ready just in case.

Their teachers may have organised a pre-exam revision session so check
this with them as they will need to be in school earlier than usual.

✓ Ask them if they need to leave for school earlier
  or later than usual and think about
  whether you need to adjust
  your routine.

✓ Make sure they have packed their
  pencil case and have got other
  items ready (watch, bus pass,
  water bottle etc).

> "Get them to pack their
> bag the night before
> with everything they'll
> need for the exam."

✓ Check they know whether the
  exam is in the morning or
  afternoon, the start time and where it is (Hall, Gym etc).

✓ Make extra allowances for the fact that they may behave differently and
  could possibly be more moody or short tempered.

On the day of an exam

Students should get up in plenty of time, perhaps a little earlier than usual,
so that they do not have to rush.

Some students like to do some last-minute revision such as flicking through
revision notes whilst others simply want to get ready to go. It is totally
normal for them to be nervous at this stage (who wouldn't be?)!

Whether you are at home or not on the day of an exam, do all you can to
ensure that things are calm.

✓ Avoid asking them how they feel or giving them last minute advice.

✓ Encourage them to have breakfast even if they usually don't.

✓ If you are taking them to school on that day make sure you are well
  organised and that you arrive in good time.

✓ Tell them to avoid people who irritate them or may talk negatively about
  the exam ahead.

✓ This is the point at which there is nothing left for you to do – they're on
  their own!

After each exam

The emotions students feel after an exam will vary enormously. After some they may feel elated (if you're lucky!) whilst after others there will be tears.

When you see them for the first time following an exam they may not want to talk about it. In fact, they may not say anything at all and just go straight to their room. If they do talk about it, listen but avoid interrogating them about the details of the exam.

✓ As tempting as it is, try not to ask them how an exam went but wait for them to say something when they're ready.
✓ Keep everything as normal as possible.

"Keep everything as normal as possible.."

Are we there yet?

Towards the end of the exam period students will get very tired and any enthusiasm they may have shown for revising will inevitably begin to wane. You too will start to flag. This is not an easy time for students taking exams or for parents looking on.

✓ Continue showing an interest, supporting them and giving plenty of praise and encouragement.
✓ Grit your teeth for one final push!

And finally...

When eventually the exams are over, it's time to celebrate! You may want to organise a special event, order their favourite takeaway or simply collapse with them in a heap on the sofa!

✓ It's time for them to look forward to a long summer holiday.
✓ It's time for you to give YOURSELF a treat!